catching fireflies

Donloyn LeDuff Gadson

Birthing Hope

Creole Magnolia Publishing

Copyright © 2020 Donloyn LeDuff Gadson
All rights reserved.
Visit the author's website at www.BirthingHope.com and www.Donloyn.com

Scripture quotations marked NKJV are taken from the New King James Version®. Copyright © 1982 by Thomas Nelson. Used by permission. All rights reserved.

Scripture quotations marked NLT are from the Holy Bible, New Living Translation, copyright © 1996, 2004, 2015 by Tyndale House Foundation. Used by permission of Tyndale House Publishers Inc., Carol Stream, Illinois 60188. All rights reserved.

Scripture quotations marked KJV are from the King James Version of the Bible.

Scripture quotations marked NIV are taken from the Holy Bible, New International Version®, NIV®. Copyright © 1973, 1978, 1984, 2011 by Biblica, Inc.™ Used by permission of Zondervan. All rights reserved worldwide. www.zondervan.com The "NIV" and "New International Version" are trademarks registered in the United States Patent and Trademark Office by Biblica, Inc.™

Scripture quotations marked TPT are from The Passion Translation®. Copyright © 2017, 2018 by Passion & Fire Ministries, Inc. Used by permission. All rights reserved. ThePassionTranslation.com.

Scripture quotations taken from the Amplified® Bible (AMP),
Copyright © 2015 by The Lockman Foundation
Used by permission. www.Lockman.org

Scripture quotations are from the ESV® Bible (The Holy Bible, English Standard Version®), copyright © 2001 by Crossway, a publishing ministry of Good News Publishers. Used by permission. All rights reserved.

2020 Creole Magnolia Publishing Trade Paperback Edition
ISBN-13: 978-0-9982952-3-7

For every woman who has ever pushed through despair to find glimmers of hope.

For every woman who is currently surrounded by night and longs for that one small flicker that will interrupt the darkness.

For every woman who refuses to allow her light to be smothered by a blanket of hopelessness but instead taps into her childlike wonder and decides to spend the rest of her life Catching Fireflies!

This book is for you.

"Hope is being able to see that there is light despite all of the darkness."

~Archbishop Desmond Tutu

Table of Contents

ACKNOWLEDGMENTS iii

PREFACE v

A POEM FOR YOU xiii

Let's Begin! 1

    FIREFLIES 3

    BIOLUMINESCENCE 9

    HOPE 15

catching fireflies 25

    POSITIONING 27

        In the Still of the Night 34

        Where the Spark Lives 36

        X Marks the Spot 38

            A Guided Journal Moment 42

    HONESTY 47

        I'm Afraid 53

        honestly…hopefully 56

            A Guided Journal Moment 59

    TRUST 63

        Footsteps of the Wind 69

Can I Trust You with My Voice?	71
Me, Myself, and I	73
A Guided Journal Moment	74
PATIENCE	**79**
I'll Dance	84
my little light	88
A Guided Journal Moment	90
HEALING	**93**
I Set This Day Before You	99
When It Rains…	102
A Guided Journal Moment	107
COURAGE	**113**
I Hear the Wind	117
I Stand	119
A Guided Journal Moment	123
EXPECTATION	**129**
The Hope Inside	134
My Dream Sings to Me	136
A Guided Journal Moment	139
OPEN JARS	**143**

ACKNOWLEDGMENTS

Literal blood, sweat, and tears—a lot of tears—are laced in between the words in this book. They dot i's, cross t's, bridge thoughts, and form ideas. As I sit here typing this, reflecting on all that brought me to this moment, my heart is bursting with gratitude…and quite honestly, a few more tears. But good ones.

First and foremost, all thanks, praises, and glory to my God in Heaven. Thank You, Jehovah. In the mighty name of Jesus, I thank You. Thank You for holding me in the palm of Your glorious hand. Thank You for carrying me when I could not bear the thought of holding myself up. Thank you for restoring me. For healing me. For escorting me down the path to healing and hope. Thank You for allowing me to feel the excitement of a physical life growing inside of me again. Although it did not end the way I had expected, You used that darkness to bring light to my life. You placed a new hope inside of me…new expectations and new hope-filled wonders to birth. You taught me how to catch fireflies! You are amazing, Father. I love You and I Thank You!

To my husband, Aastan. Words cannot express how much I love you. We have been through so much together. After we lost our baby, you focused on nurturing and nursing me back to health. You held me when I cried and listened to my angry rants when I could not make sense of all we were experiencing. You were my rock. The one I could talk to. The one who allowed me the space to feel and express without judgment. You did not try to "make" me feel better. You supported me as I got better. But during that time, my heart ached for you. I often wondered about your wounds and how deeply they really went. And although we wept together once, you are the type of man who processes quietly. My prayer is and has always been that for every bit of love and tenderness you poured into me that God would multiply that exponentially and pour it back into you. You have been by my side for every good thing that has come from our tragedy. And for that I say thank you.

PREFACE

I want to take a moment to share the reason behind the creating of this book.

As this book is being written and published, it is currently the year 2020. If you are reading this ten, twenty, thirty years from now, or beyond, then you likely understand the significance of this statement as this year has been marked by circumstances that have had long lasting, global impacts.

Historically, 2020 will be remembered as a somber year, evidenced by the COVID-19 pandemic; quarantine and isolation; massive loss of life; racial, political, and social unrest; unemployment and shutdowns, and disappointments seemingly at every turn. Not to mention the darkness and pain felt in the lives of many on a personal level.

For me, the year 2020 began with grand promises of Hope. Hope was my focus word for the year, given to me directly from The LORD. I became a student of Hope. I immersed myself in scriptures and quotes surrounding it. I journaled about it. I wrote poems about it. I had conversations about it. I even taught three sessions at a women's conference in January that centered around it.

I planted it like seeds in the rich soil of my heart. And, as its blooms burst forth, Hope and all its fragrant beauty permeated every area of my life.

On January 19, 2020, we received news of the most beautiful "Hope Bloom" of all...I was pregnant! At the time, I was 47 and a mother of 8. So, after the initial shock, we were ecstatic! Hope was having its way with us, and I was experiencing joy on a whole new level.

I had a knowing in my heart that the unexpected life growing inside of me was a gift...a seed and a promise of Hope. A glimmer of pure light.

I was happy...filled with an indescribable joy. We all were! We were making plans and tossing around ideas. Chatter of a new house and possible room assignments floated between the kids. We even settled on a name...Julianna Hope Gadson, "J-Hope" for short! My husband even began plans to design and build her cradle.

But sadly, plans for a custom-made cradle and dreams of holding our precious girl came to screeching halt.

On March 1, 2020, I miscarried our sweet Hope. Our lives were turned upside down and my heart was shattered. Every bloom of Hope in my life seemed to die, simultaneously. Every light was replaced with a deep darkness. Despair gripped me. And I thought I would never stop crying.

The loss of the baby hit me hard. I found myself in a state of uncertainty and doubt...an emotional, mental, and spiritual quandary. I could not reconcile the miscarriage of my pregnancy with all the promises The LORD had spoken and confirmed to me. When I placed those promises next to my reality, there was no equal sign in between. The equation was imbalanced. Something did not add up.

I began to ask The LORD questions. Hard questions. I began searching for wisdom and understanding. And I did so with honesty. Honesty with myself and honesty with God.

I did not speak with anyone but my husband and children. I was not ready to talk and had zero interest in hearing any meaningless platitudes. Interestingly, during that time, the coronavirus began to spread across the United States, and we were instructed to quarantine. The forced isolation had no effect on me as I had already deliberately walled myself off from friends and family. I was fine with being closed in. All I wanted was answers. And those answers needed to come from God.

Those answers came. They came in the form of one word…

HOPE.

There was that word again. Isn't that just like God to take you right back to the place He needed you to be all along.

In re-hearing that word, I realized I had equated its meaning with that of Joy and Happiness. I was reminded of its true definition. I was reminded of its power. I was reminded that I was to cling to that word in its entirety. And what better time to cling to Hope than when things seem hopeless.

The LORD also brought me to this scripture at Hosea 2:14,15:

> "Therefore I am now going to allure her;
> I will lead her into the wilderness
> and speak tenderly to her.
> There I will give her back her vineyards,
> and will make the Valley of Achor [or the Valley of Trouble] a

> *door of hope.*
> *There she will respond [or sing] as in the days of her youth,*
> *as in the day she came up out of Egypt."*

This scripture is a perfect depiction of where I was. I was literally lured and led into an emotional and spiritual wilderness. That sounds harsh, but this scripture is filled with promise! It is filled with HOPE! This scripture says He will speak tenderly to me, give me back my vineyards, and make this Valley of Trouble a doorway of Hope!

I was in a dark and desolate place…a night season. And God was promising me fireflies! He was promising to send me glimmers of Hope!

As I sat in my darkness, I meditated on scriptures. I prayed. I cried. I worshiped. I pressed in. I processed. I dealt with the emotional crud that began to surface because of the loss. I did the dirty work. And all the while, I held on tightly to the promise of Hope. Hebrews 11:1 says, "Faith is the substance of things hoped for, the evidence of things unseen." Even though all I could see around me was darkness, I chose Hope.

As I did so, I began to see the glimmers. I began to see the glimmers of Hope. Fireflies began to light up the darkness that had tried so desperately to suffocate me.

A shift took place. A light literally came on! Healing happened, and I was able to not just hold on to the thought of hope, but I was able to do it! I was able to hope again! I was able to feel light and promise and joy despite the circumstances I had experienced.

After this breakthrough, God placed an urgent desire within me to share the process He took me through. And with that urgency came this title: *Catching Fireflies: a 7 Step Poetic Guide to Capturing Glimmers of Hope.* The name of this book filled my spirit, and now, here it is…in your hands. Allow Him to minister to you through its pages. Let Him show you how to capture glimmers of Hope the same way He showed me.

Perhaps you are reading this book because of a dark period that occurred in 2020 or perhaps some other moment in time. The year does not matter. This formula is timeless. This 7-step journey to bringing light and hope to your darkness can be embarked upon at any time in your life.

Many are marking this as a year of bad luck and hardship. But that is not so! It does not have to be. I could have given up. I could have given in. I could have allowed my loss to define what life looked like for me moving forward. I did not! I chose the opposite.

And now, what once appeared to be one of the worst years of my life has been turned into one of the most prosperous. The year that was once marked by death and darkness has now been bathed in life and light!

Here's a glimmer of hope for you: *Anything that is meant to destroy you, God will use it to teach you, heal you, grow you, bless you and lift you up, if... and only if... you let Him!*

May God bless you as you learn the art of *Catching Fireflies!*

A POEM FOR YOU

"Catching Fireflies"

When I was young, I took the time
to sit in stillness and catch fireflies
to wander without fear, dreaming in the dark
sheer excitement and wonder with just one spark

the warm and sticky feel of the night
the environment was exactly right
...a good time for catching fireflies

As I got older, life turned strange
marred by hurts, disappointments, and change
eyes tight, fists clenched, fighting for a breath
fearful of the darkness and its real threat of death

its depths were deep as I went down, down, down
only thing left to do was drown
...a good time for catching fireflies

Life has taught me valuable lessons
And surprised me with many unexpected blessings

DONLOYN LEDUFF GADSON

I have learned no matter the length of your rope
when you come to its end there is always hope

capturing glimmers at night is an art
whether darkness outside or the depths of your heart
…it's always a good time for catching fireflies

Explore these pages with soul wide open
and receive the message within this poem
get in position and open your jar
this book is living, a flying star

a bug of lightning to guide your way
to lead you from night to the brightest day
…this is the time for catching fireflies

Let's Begin!

"The only impossible journey is the one you never begin."

~Tony Robbins

DONLOYN LEDUFF GADSON

<u>FIREFLIES</u>

"Hurry come see this!"

These are the words I exclaimed one evening while on a camping trip with my husband and kids. I could not believe my eyes.

I was beaming with excitement.

It was a dark, cold November night in South Carolina. I was headed back to our campsite from the campground bathrooms. In my hand…a small LED lantern to light my way.

As I was walking, tiny flickers of light in a nearby tree caught my eyes. A breathless excitement washed over me, and my heart began to race.

"There are fireflies everywhere!" I shouted.

It had been years since I had seen a firefly. And here, this tree was filled with what appeared to be hundreds!

I gathered my family, and, after grabbing a few more lanterns, we quickly headed toward what could only be described as nature's awesome lightshow.

As we approached the tree and the dozens upon dozens of glimmering specks, my husband shared a disappointing, yet hysterical, revelation. Much to my dismay, those tiny flickers were not fireflies, at all. They were flashing Christmas lights from a neighboring campsite that were casting their glow on the tree above. HA! Christmas lights!

My husband teased and chuckled as we all laughed uncontrollably. But if I am honest…a small part of me felt let down. Let down that what I had perceived to be a fantastic wonder that would have undoubtedly been recorded in my children's minds as one of their fondest memories was nothing magical, at all. But, despite the bit of sadness I felt in that moment, I made up my mind to go on pretending that the lights were indeed fireflies. And my daughters were content to play along.

Fireflies are enchanting! We see their presence in childhood movies and storybooks. From that, we discern that they are the essence from which great fairytales are written and told. We recall past moments of chasing them on warm summer nights. Those precious memories prove that they are illusive creatures that require you to be in the right place at the right time just to get a glimpse of their breathtaking glow. A glow that gives the observer permission to dream…wildly, vividly, and freely.

Some folks call them lightning bugs. Some call them glow worms. But interestingly, they are not flies, bugs, or worms, at all. They are beetles.

Closely related to ladybugs and Japanese beetles, the wings of these whimsical wonders are protected by a hard, outer shell. And that is not all they have in common with their flying cousins. They also go through a growth process known as complete metamorphosis. Complete metamorphosis refers to the series of changes that the firefly goes and grows through during its lifetime.

Fireflies begin as eggs, laid underground. They, then, develop into larvae that appear as lumpy worm-like creatures. Surprisingly, they glow even during these early stages of development. After a year, the larvae transition into the pupa stage. This is the phase in the firefly's life cycle when it undergoes internal changes necessary to look like the fireflies we see.

In the pupa stage, the larvae settle in chambers they create in the mud. Some species even attach themselves to bark and hang upside down, much like caterpillars. It is during this time the larva is broken down and made over into its adult form. The newly formed firefly emerges from the pupa, marking the beginning of adulthood. Fireflies only live about a month or two after reaching this point. Just long enough to mate, lay eggs and continue the life cycle.

Fireflies—known by their scientific name Lampyridae, which means "shining fire" or "to shine like a lamp"—have an interesting diet. In its glowing larva stage, it partakes in an underground, carnivorous feast of worms, slugs, and snails. As they advance to their adult stage, their diet changes quite a bit. As adults, they consume considerably less nourishment, if any at all. Scientists believe this is due to their limited lifespan once they reach this phase. Adult fireflies are generally more concerned with mating and reproducing during this time. However, if they do eat, their diet may consist of pollen, nectar and, because they are carnivorous, even other fireflies. This cannibalistic behavior is interesting, as they are not known to consume any other type of insect at this stage.

Yes, fireflies are insects. And like all insects, they are six-legged creatures consisting of three main body parts: head, thorax, and abdomen. However, the abdomen on the firefly has an added feature. Positioned just below the abdomen is the unique body part that produces the firefly's mesmerizing glow…the lantern.

You may be wondering why, in a book about hope, I am sharing the physiological details of the firefly with you. I am sharing these things because, not only are fireflies magical, they are also symbolic. For you to successfully embark upon this poetic journey, you must understand how meaningful these luminous creatures are. And that requires some basic knowledge about their natural makeup.

So, keep turning the pages as I share a little more about our fiery friends.

BIOLUMINESCENCE

There is nothing quite as wondrous and stimulating as the glow of the firefly. Itsq fantastic flashing invites passersby to settle in for a private performance. As they light, they strike up a silent symphony that showcases a poetic percussion, causing a rhythm to beat and pulsate from the darkness. A secret serenade that, undoubtedly, stirs up a charming fascination in the heart and mind of the spectator.

But what causes this amazing light? How is something this majestic possible?

This glow is called Bioluminescence. Bioluminescence is the biochemical emission of light from a living organism. If we break the word into its parts, we can clearly see its meaning.

bio + lumin + essence = bioluminescence

bio: life; pertaining to living organisms; one's life course or way of living

lumin: light, brightness

essence: process or state of being; beginning, becoming or tending to be

Therefore, bioluminescence is a state or process in which a living thing gives off light. (Hint: Remember this for later!)

And while scientists are not sure how these brilliant beauties control their glow, they do know how the glow is produced. The firefly's lantern, located at the end of its abdomen, contains a chemical called luciferin (which means "light bringer") and an enzyme called luciferase.

> *NOTE: *You may have noticed the similarity between the words luciferin and luciferase and the enemy we know as Lucifer. Do not be alarmed by this. Before he was cast down, Satan was known in Heaven as the angel Lucifer. The meaning of his name was "light bringer." He was known as the "son of the morning." We can assume that when he was in right standing with God, he was an angel of light. The Bible also tells us to be wise and aware of Satan's tricks, as he can appear to us as an angel of light — a trait that he no longer uses for good.*

"How you are fallen from heaven, O Lucifer, son of the morning [light bringer]! How you are cut down to the ground, you who weakened the nations!"

Isaiah 14:12, NKJV

"And no wonder! For Satan himself transforms himself into an angel of light."
II Corinthians 11:14, NKJV

When oxygen enters the lantern, it mixes with luciferin, luciferase, calcium, and adenosine triphosphate (ATP), a compound that produces energy in living things. This coming together creates the chemical reaction that we call bioluminescence, and light is produced.

But the light that is created from our bioluminescent buddies is not ordinary light. It is unique! Fireflies are 100% light givers. This means the light they produce is the most efficient source of light energy in existence since zero percent is lost as heat. 100% of the energy produced by a firefly is pure light! Comparatively, an incandescent lightbulb only produces 10% light, losing the remaining 90% as heat. Fluorescent lights come close by producing 90% light and only losing 10% as heat, but they are still no match for nature's light geniuses.

Now that we know how they produce their captivating glow, one question remains…why do they do it at all?

Fireflies light up the night sky for three main reasons, and all three of the following come down to communication:

1. **Protection**: Fireflies use their flashing to communicate with predators. They contain a defensive steroid call lucibufagins that carries an

unpleasant taste. Predators associate this awful taste with the firefly's glow and know to stay away.

2. **Identification**: Fireflies use their glow to communicate with other fireflies. Through synchronized flashing, they can identify other Lampyridae from the same species.

3. **Flirtation**: Fireflies use their flashing to communicate with prospective mates. The male firefly uses a specific pattern of "fiery" sweet talk to attract females. If a female of his species is enticed by his glowing pursuit, then she will respond with a special glow of her own. They recognize this exchange as being exclusive to the two of them. It is basically a private, flirty Morse Code!

Sadly, there is a real threat against this bioluminescent world. As mesmerizing as these nocturnal night lights are, their numbers are declining. Light pollution, pesticide use, and habitat destruction have become real dangers to their existence.

(Again…remember this!)

Now that I have laid a well-lit foundation regarding our friend the firefly, it is time to illuminate this information in a way that will shine a new light and reveal a fresh meaning.

So, keep turning the pages…here comes that symbolism I promised.

HOPE

Hope.

I believe the power and significance of this small four-letter word are lost on most. We see the word tossed about so often in its casual use that we become desensitized to the real weight it carries.

Hope, for many, is as simple as saying, "I hope we don't have a pop quiz in Biology class today;" "I hope it doesn't rain tomorrow," or, "I hope my husband remembers to swing by the store on his way home from work."

And while these illustrations are technically correct, they do not adequately convey the gravity of the word.

For me, hope is what I clung to when one of our twin sons was born with a birth defect that required two major surgeries to repair—one at 5 weeks old and one at 5 months.

Hope, for me, is what gave me the strength to push forward each day when my husband was hit with a rare illness that caused him to be hospitalized for 2 months and forced him to endure countless hours of outpatient therapy, not to mention how the experience shook our family and rattled our foundation.

Hope is what sustained me when I began hemorrhaging after the birth of our twin daughters, resulting in the paramedics rushing me back to the hospital. I did not know if I would live or die. Fortunately, I did not hold fast to what I did or did not know. I held on to hope.

Hope is the basket I used to collect the shattered bits of my heart after I miscarried our baby girl. Hope is the adhesive that glued those bits together again. Hope is what dried the tears and held my hands as I was escorted from heartbreak to healing.

Hope, for me, is the small glimmer of light when you are shrouded by darkness.

Hope, for me, is the firefly. The majestic glow in what appears to be a darkened forest of despair.

It is when the stars come down from the night sky and settle amid a desolate world, bringing a light that promises that full sun will one day come again.

It is the flickering of Christmas lights from a nearby campsite, shining into a tree, masquerading as community of fireflies. It is the childlike willingness to pretend those manmade lights are nature's bright wonder.

Hope is when you are lost in a darkened spiritual, emotional, and mental wilderness and you rely on small twinkles of brightness to guide you home.

Those twinkles are hope.

And hope is a firefly.

I love how God uses creation to speak to us. That fact alone gives us hope. The symbolism that can be found in a river, a butterfly, a mountain, a tree or even a firefly has the divine ability to breathe life into us when we are teetering on the verge of lifelessness.

There are so many hope-inspired symbols around us. We need only look. However, none of these images has the innate ability of capturing the essence of hope quite as magically as the firefly.

Let me ask you something. When do we see fireflies? We see fireflies when we are outside, surrounded by complete darkness, positioned with our eyes open. The same is true for hope. Hope does not surface when everything around us is going smoothly. Hope is reserved for those moments of fear, uncertainty, and doubt. Hope is the little light in the pitch-black tunnel that we follow to freedom. Hope is that upon which faith is built. Hope is the courage to invest in a reality we cannot yet see.

"Now faith is the substance of things hoped for, the evidence of things not seen."

~Hebrews 11:1, NKJV

So just as we sit still in the night with our eyes open in order to catch a glimpse of the firefly, we must also quietly position ourselves in the darkness of our circumstances and open the eyes of our hearts, minds and spirits in order to capture glimmers of hope. When we step outside of our situations and still ourselves long enough in our own personal darkness, we see that there is light inside. Yes, we possess glimmers of light…glimmers of hope are a part of us. They reside in our spirits. The fireflies are within.

"for you are all sons of light and sons of day. We do not belong to the night nor to darkness. So then let us not sleep [in spiritual indifference] as the rest [of the world does] but let us keep wide awake [alert and cautious] and let us be sober [self-controlled, calm, and wise]. For those who sleep, sleep at night, and those who are drunk get drunk at night. But since we [believers] belong to the day, let us be sober, having put on the breastplate of faith and love, and as a helmet, the hope and confident assurance of salvation."

1 Thessalonians 5: 5-8, AMP

For the entirety of its life—from egg to adult—the firefly shines. They are creatures of light. As are we. We are called sons or children of light.

Fireflies are also nocturnal, remaining wide awake and alert in the night. The aforementioned scripture says we ought to do the same. We are to be awake and cautious during times and seasons of darkness.

Another parallel that can be drawn between us and fireflies is our composition. Fireflies have 3 main body parts: head, thorax, and abdomen. Similarly, we, too, are comprised of 3 parts: mind, body, and spirit. The firefly has an extra element or extension of their abdomen called the lantern—the place where the magic happens. We, as believers of God and followers of Christ, also have an added element.

"Once more Jesus addressed the crowd. He said, 'I am the Light of the world. He who follows Me will not walk in the darkness, but will have the Light of life.'"

John 8:12, AMP

When we walk in union with The Father and His Son, Jesus Christ, we walk in His Light. Our "lanterns" come from the light of The Holy Spirit and are powered by God's word which is light. When our spirits operate with the Spirit of God, we carry His Light. And when we carry His Light, we can tap into hope for ourselves as well as be a source of hope for others.

So, if we are likened to the firefly because of our ability to emit light, then this means that we are also bioluminescent — living beings who radiate light, and thus, radiate hope.

"…so that you may prove yourselves to be blameless and guileless, innocent and uncontaminated, children of God without blemish in the midst of a [morally] crooked and [spiritually] perverted generation, among whom you are seen as bright lights [beacons shining out clearly] in the world [of darkness]…"

Philippians 2:15, AMP

"Now may God, the inspiration and fountain of hope, fill you to overflowing with uncontainable joy and perfect peace as you trust in him. And may the power of the Holy Spirit continually surround your life with his super-abundance until you radiate with hope!"

Romans 15:13, TPT

Our similarities with this glowing marvel do not end here. Just as the firefly undergoes complete metamorphosis, we, as children of God, experience significant internal changes of our own. And like the firefly, these changes take place in darkness.

If you recall, when it is time for firefly larvae to advance to the adult phase, they go into mud chambers underground where they are melted down and reconstructed into the adult firefly we have come to admire. Darkness is part of the growth process for us, as well. If we approach with the proper perspective, it is during these personal times of darkness when we are transformed for the better.

How, then, do we approach our challenging situations with the proper perspective so that we can be certain change will occur? We feast on meat! Remember, during its time in the larva stage, the firefly indulges in a carnivorous feast of worms, grubs, and snails. When it enters its mud chamber — the dark place where its complete metamorphosis takes place — it is well nourished. Now, it can be sustained both during its transformation and after, when it goes forth to do its job of continuing the cycle of creating more fireflies.

The same is true for us. The Word of God is meat, and we are to feast on it so that, during times of darkness, we have the nourishment we need to facilitate the transformation of our hearts and minds. We also need to consume God's word so that we, like the firefly, can be equipped to carry out

God's plans for our lives, which includes continuing the Kingdom lifecycle of making disciples of others.

While we are on the topic of diet, please call to mind the fact that adult fireflies sometimes eat other insects. Interestingly, when they do, they usually eat other fireflies, making them cannibals. Here is yet another trait we have in common with our bioluminescent besties! Let me explain…If we are light and we consume the Word of God, which is also light, then, in a way, we are cannibals, too! Light eating Light!

When we are in proper alignment with The Father—like the firefly—the light we emit is also 100% pure light. It is powerful and capable of illuminating the entire world. Again, like the firefly, we use our light to communicate…with other believers, with those who do not know God and, most importantly, with God Himself.

"You are the light of the world. A city that is set on a hill cannot be hidden. Nor do they light a lamp and put it under a basket, but on a lampstand, and it gives light to all who are in the house. Let your light so shine before men, that they may see your good works and glorify your Father in heaven."

Matthew 5: 14-16, NKJV

As beacons of hope, there are real threats against our light, also. Fireflies are threatened by light pollution. The equivalent for us would be the threat of a false light or failing to tap into the true light of God. As God's children, we must be aware of false prophets and deceptions of the enemy. Remember, Satan can disguise himself as an angel of light. If we are rooted in the true light, then we cannot be duped by any imposter.

The life of the firefly is also jeopardized by pesticides. Pesticides for the believer would be anything deadly the enemy sends to stop, kill, or interrupt the will of God in our lives. Distractions, disappointments, setbacks, fear, depression are all examples of pesticides that are used against us…the list could go on. The enemy comes to steal, kill, and destroy our light, but Christ came that we might have life (and hope) and have it more abundantly (John 10:10).

The third danger we face that is parallel to the dangers that fireflies confront is the threat of habitat destruction. Ask yourself this question…*Where am I abiding?* Are you abiding in Christ? Are you making His Presence your home? If the distractions and troubles of life can keep you from resting and abiding in him, then your light will be snuffed out. And all attempts to capture glimmers of hope in the darkness will fail.

Now that you see the connection between hope, the firefly, and us, let us begin our 7-step, poetic journey. Let us pick up the open jars of our hearts and minds, step out into the darkness of our circumstances, position ourselves with spiritual eyes wide open, and catch a few glimmers of hope!

> *NOTE: Journaling is important during this time. Recording your thoughts, ideas and emotions is a crucial part of any discovery process. So, grab a journal and write any revelations or hope-filled inspirations you may receive!*

catching fireflies

a 7 Step Poetic Guide to capturing Glimmers of Hope

STEP 1

POSITIONING

―――――――――――――――――

"Learning how to be still, to really be still and let life happen - that stillness becomes a radiance."

~Morgan Freeman

STEP 1

<u>A TIME OF POSITIONING</u>

Recently, I took a road trip from South Carolina to Missouri with my family. My husband drove. And while it sounds relaxing to be able to sit back and enjoy the open road, this has always been a source of stress for me. Not because my husband is a poor driver, but because I am a poor passenger. It is difficult for me to "be still" and "let life happen" when someone else is in control of the wheel. Over two decades of marriage and I am still a work-in-progress.

Our route to Missouri took us through the mountainous regions of North Carolina and Tennessee. Seeing the Blue Ridge and Great Smoky Mountains was a thing of beauty. But, oddly, it was, also, both intimidating and humbling. The height and grandeur of the elevations called into question the size of my presence. The scale of my existence felt threatened, and my largeness — or should I say lack thereof — was brought into proper perspective. The reality of my smallness, coupled with being driven by someone else down serpentine twists and turns of mountainous highways, brought out a strange anxiety I had never experienced. My hand gripped the door handle tightly as I firmly pressed an imaginary brake pedal on the floorboard beneath me. My heart raced as I inhaled deeply and diligently focused my thoughts and my breath.

The road snaked and twisted between massive rocks like an elaborate racecar track. And after what felt like the one millionth chicane, I arrived at a few conclusions. In that moment, not only had I come face-to-face with the realization that the space I take up is small, but also with the awareness of my incessant need for control and the understanding that that need will never be met.

Human beings seem to be wired with the misconception that we are in control of everything. But the reality is, the only thing we are in control of are our individual responses to the world around us. That is so important it bears repeating: *The only thing we are in control of are our individual responses to the world around us. We can only control how we respond.*

Exercising control over our responses to life events in a meaningful way requires positioning—a deliberate, well-executed time of contemplative stillness.

As we were driving down unfamiliar roads lined with warning signs to watch for fallen rock, I had to decide to still myself. In order to overcome the anxiety and fear that was brewing, I had to position myself.

The same is true when we are in search of that proverbial firefly. When we are searching for light in our seasons of blackness, we must be willing to be still…to position ourselves. Positioning requires simultaneously stepping outside of the situation while sitting completely still inside of it.

But what does that mean?

Stepping outside of the situation signifies a shift in your perspective. It means removing your emotions from the situation long enough to see the big picture and all its details. Only then can you posture yourself—still, motionless, with eyes wide open—amid your circumstances.

It is a choice…a delicate process involving both the mind and heart. Stepping outside of your situation is a conscious act that occurs in the mind, while remaining "still" inside the situation happens in the heart. It is a quieting of your soul and a tapping into your spirit as you rest in your circumstance.

Stillness and quietude are terrifying. It can be scary, and quite uncomfortable, to allow yourself to sit in the total darkness of your situation. However, there is a hope that is waiting to reveal itself in the dark…a firefly ready to flash. But you will not see it if you are not properly positioned.

> *"I will take my post; I will position myself on the fortress. I will keep watch to see what the Lord says to me and how he will respond to my complaint."*
>
> *Habakkuk 2:1*

How can we know what The Lord will say or how He will respond if we do not sit still with Him in the midnight hours of our lives? How can we watch Him fight our battles if we are not correctly postured?

By positioning myself during the car ride, I was able to overcome fear and tap into a light that drove out the darkness of anxiety. And though this illustration is not one that is life-altering, it is representative of how positioning yourself in smaller situations can prepare and train you to do the same in ones that may be darker and more intense — in my case, healing from the death of our unborn child.

During the days and weeks following our miscarriage, I made a conscious decision to position myself. My healing was contingent upon my response to the situation. Here I was fully immersed in lugubrious emotion — feeling no relief, thinking I would never stop crying—and yet, I found the strength to step outside of my pain while simultaneously quieting myself in the midst of it.

This was hard. This **IS** hard. But we can do hard things.

I am proof that God will send a firefly in the darkness. He will send a ray of hope into your bleakest situation. But you must decide to position yourself and be still. The decision to respond productively in hard situations is the only control we possess.

"You will not need to fight in this battle. Position yourselves, stand still and see the salvation of the LORD, who is with you, O Judah and Jerusalem! Do not fear or be dismayed; tomorrow go out against them, for the LORD is with you."

II Chronicles 20:17, NKJV

In the Still of the Night

in the still of the night
in solitude, I sit in secret
in the quiet of my soul
where fireflies often frequent
I wait for them to take flight
in the still of the night

in the still of the night
I am perfectly positioned
to receive a glimmer of hope
my heart eager to be conditioned
I look for the light
in the still of the night

in the still of the night
I take refuge from the darkness
under a vast canopy of uncertainty
I find safety from the blackness
I await divine sight
in the still of the night

in the still of the night

my spirit erects a sacred sanctuary

shielded by an army of well-lit friends

their illumination pierces my adversary

I am equipped for the fight

in the still of the night

in the still of the night

I am completely at home

we abide in one another

I am never alone

He is the light

so, I am safe, in the still of the night

Where the Spark Lives

Positioning is more

than the placement of your feet

it is the posture of the heart

that is crying for release

it is walking through the jungle

and forest of your mind

and finding that special spot

that no one else can find

it is remaining in that space as long as it takes

knowing what is promised is worth the wait

it is sitting on the dance floor

anticipating music to start

with expectant eyes lifted high

waiting for the ball to spark

it is silencing the noise

and allowing your heart to speak

settling into the vast unknown

and finally finding peace

it is the ability to be in a crowded place

yet finding that pocket of protection

stepping into the innermost room

for divine rendezvous and connection

it is boldly accepting the invitation

to willingly step into darkness

awaiting the loosing of fireflies

in the blackness is where the spark lives

X Marks the Spot

I flip through memories
And go back in time
saddened by some of the things I find
A treasure trove of report cards
divided in charts
Each sectioned off
In boxes and slots
received good feedback
On academics taught
But in the space labeled "self-control"
X marks the spot

A little girl struggling
A victim of crime
Survival was sadly
The only thing on my mind
Every negative comment
Felt like tiny darts
bleeding inside
a soul filled with clots
Not working well with others

broke rules and fought
And in the space "accepts responsibility"
X marks the spot

I wish I could tell you
Of a girl who was free
To catch fire in jars
And climb high up in trees
Instead, the girl
was bossy and bold
a pirate plundering
zero self-control
as my eyes skim over
other behavior slots
I see missed inflection points
X marks the spot

Many crucial moments
were denoted with an X
I'll share a few here
I'll try to do my best

When darkness was multiplied

Night times black

When my answers were wrong
False versus fact

When rejection hung a sign
Don't enter, turn back

When I realized my infinite dimensions
Grand impact

When I promised to be fearless
And never fall back

When I saw inside a buried treasure
My life an elaborate map

In all these spaces an X inked in black

this reflection uncovered
each X once concealed
so I sat still in uncertainty

So light could be revealed

A light that produces

Healing through transition

But the healing is only promised

To those in correct position

so I sit...

Positioned...

awaiting the lifting of dark...

I sit...

Positioned...

X marks the spot

A Guided Journal Moment:

ON POSITIONING

Being assigned the Augean task of posturing yourself in stillness — in the center of darkness — is likely bringing about some anxiety, but the payoff is worth it.

Quiet yourself. Find a private space and consider the following prompts. Write your responses in a personal journal or in the spaces provided here.

* *What situation in your life is currently presenting itself as a time of darkness…a time where a glimmer of hope is needed?*

  _____
  _____
  _____
  _____
  _____
  _____
  _____
  _____
  _____
  _____

- *Are you willing to position yourself in this time of darkness to capture a glimmer of hope?*

_____
_____
_____
_____
_____

- *How have you been responding to this situation? Have you been attempting to control the world and/or others around you?*

_____
_____
_____
_____
_____
_____
_____
_____
_____
_____
_____
_____
_____

Consider the poem "X Marks the Spot." Now, take a moment to reflect on your life. Do you see patterns of attempting to control situations and/or others while failing to control yourself? If so, what is your earliest recollection? Do you think identifying patterns of resistance to positioning can help you focus on controlling your response to life circumstances?

_____
_____
_____
_____
_____
_____
_____
_____
_____
_____
_____
_____
_____
_____
_____
_____
_____

Step outside of your current situation. Remove your emotions momentarily and examine it objectively. How can you better your response? How can you control your own thoughts and actions?

STEP 2

HONESTY

"Honesty is often very hard. The truth is often painful. But the freedom it can bring is worth the trying."

~Fred Rogers

STEP 2

<u>A TIME OF HONESTY</u>

There are fewer things as challenging as honesty. But nothing we do is worth doing if it is not done in truth. And that requires being honest with others, with God and, ultimately, with ourselves. And admitting truth to self is often the most difficult.

Finding hope in a dark season requires honesty. It is scary, but there is no way around it. Honesty is a crucial element in the hope process. To capture glimmers of light in dark situations, you must be willing to tell truth, speak truth, love truth and live truth.

There is nothing about the dark that makes us want to tell the truth. We lie to ourselves in the dark. We cover our eyes and convince ourselves that the things we see are not there. Just like a child with the bed covers drawn over her face, we find comfort in hiding. Hiding behind a lie.

But we must pull the blanket away from our eyes and allow truth to reveal itself. Allow hard truths to rise to the surface. Because as they are faced and processed, light begins to peek through.

There is a bright refreshing that comes with honesty. That is, both telling the truth and knowing The Truth. It is a freedom that brings release. It lifts the heaviness of the night from your shoulders.

"And you shall know the truth, and the truth shall make you free."

John 8:32, NKJV

"Jesus said to him, 'I am the way, the truth, and the life. No one comes to the Father except through Me."

John 14:6, NKJV

When I was in search of hope after my miscarriage, I had to get honest with God and with myself. I had to be forthright regarding my emotions and pain. My freedom depended on it. I had to reveal the truth of my emotions to Jesus — who is The Truth — so that I could be set free. That is a scary thing to do.

Despite the fear, I allowed myself to be straightforward. I asked the difficult questions. When I was mad, I admitted it. I told God I was angry. When I felt betrayed by Him, I told Him. It was hard to do, but I did not pretend to be the gracious daughter of God who said all the spiritually correct things she was expected to say. Instead, I spoke the truth that was on my heart. No matter how gritty and raw those thoughts and emotions were.

Do not misunderstand. I did not disrespect The LORD, but I also did not insult His omniscience by pretending everything was okay. I walked through the darkness of my grief with vulnerability and truth. And because of that, He joined me along the way.

After I committed to a time of honesty, buried truths began to resurface. I was shocked by that. Here I was thinking I needed to confront the pain of my miscarriage only to be hit with the revelation that I had not completely dealt with all my past junk. The ruins of some of the giants I had fought and slain were still strewn about on the battlefield of my heart and mind. Simply put…I had put in the valiant work of battling past issues, but I had not rolled up my sleeves and done the dirty work of cleaning up the remains.

Let me illustrate it this way…it is like killing a spider on the wall but not cleaning up its dead body and then walking by it for weeks, avoiding the black smudge as if it is not there. And the truth is if you ignore something long enough, you will eventually lie to yourself about its existence — you will become blind to it.

Positioning myself in the pain of my miscarriage opened my eyes to some untruths I had been telling myself. Because I had not swept up the carcasses of all the beasts I had fought and defeated, I had to revisit some old wounds. I had to examine my heart. I had to come face-to-face with some old demons like unforgiveness, rejection and offense. And again, that was scary.

So, today, I challenge you to be honest. Push past the fear and discomfort and be honest with yourself. Tell God the truth. Explore your vulnerabilities. The LORD already knows what you are feeling. So, tell Him.

If you are struggling to be honest, ask yourself this…*Do I want to be held captive in this darkness? Or do I want to be free?*

Honesty is that freedom. Honesty is one step closer to hope and light…one step closer to catching fireflies.

I'm Afraid

I'm afraid…

Afraid of falling

So, I decide to just remain down

Down here

Stuck in the dark, dank pit

Of despair

I'm afraid…

Afraid of loving

So, I decide to close the doors

Of my heart

And lock myself away

On the inside

I'm afraid…

Afraid to feel joy

So, I decide to keep my floors

Bare and cold

So, the rug can never be

Pulled out from under me again

I'm afraid…

Afraid of moving forward

So, I decide to remain stalled out

On the side of this fast-paced

Road called life

It's safer on the shoulder

I'm afraid…

Afraid of trusting again

So, I decide to encapsulate

My shattered heart

It's the only way to hold

Together its fractured fragments and pieces

I'm afraid…

Afraid to talk

So, I decide to remain silent

Because I might say too much

I'm afraid…

Afraid to stop crying

So, I decide to continue

Because a lifetime of tears is better than

The threat of never feeling anything again

I'm afraid…

Afraid to keep living

So, I decide to die inside

How can I move on without you

As if you were never here

I'm afraid…

Afraid to hope

Because you were my hope

And that hope was taken away

honestly...hopefully

Sitting out here
just me and You
on this hot summer night
surrounded by the darkened sludge
'bout lost my will to fight
got this glass jar in my hand
but ain't nary a flicker in sight
    nothing left to do
        but share my truth with you
            honestly...hopefully

I have questions
plaguing my heart and mind
not quite sure where to begin
I got all excited but You let me down
much to my chagrin
I thought You said I'd never lose
with You I'd always win
    my heart is bruised
        I'm pouring out to You
            honestly...hopefully

You said one thing
yet did another
I must have heard You wrong
clouds of misery overshadowed me

and stripped me of my song
lost my footing, wandering spirit
no place where I belong
    I hurt deep inside
        but I'm sharing my mind
            honestly…hopefully

Shallow voices
add depth to the pain
words dripping with platitudes
anguish pressing, holding me down
drowning under the weight of lassitude
pulled down deeper, cannot breathe
the anchor is my attitude
    it's cutting off my air
        I'm praying You care
            honestly…hopefully

Asking questions
they say are wrong
confronting the truth in vain
confused, crushed, asking "Why?"
reconciling the promise with the pain
accusing Your word of being a lie
going completely against my grain
    I feel completely abandoned
        but I'm trying to be candid
            honestly…hopefully

Every question I asked
and comment I made
brought me back to the promise of hope
I realized the darkened hills of life
can lead to a slippery slope
with eyes closed, I focused on You
Your light formed a kaleidoscope
    so I let down my guard
        and opened my jar
            honestly…hopefully

A Guided Journal Moment:

ON HONESTY

There is a vulnerability that comes with honestly bearing one's truth. Exposing the deep emotions of your heart can be likened to revealing your weaknesses and shortcomings. It is a divulging of your soft spots and fragility. But when we are weak, He is strong. In our weaknesses, God takes the lead and His power is made perfect within us. Surrendering to a time of honesty shows you acknowledge your inability to get through the darkness on your own.

God wants us to trust Him with our truths. He wants us to be honest about our hurts and pains. He wants to build relationships with us that are free from any coverups, falsehoods or pretense. Being honest with God creates intimacy. When we share the intimate places of our hearts, we make way for hope.

* *Do you want to continue to be held captive or do you want to be free? Like, really free?*

_____

_____

_____

_____

* *Are you willing to face the truth and share that truth with Jehovah God?*

_____
_____
_____
_____

* *What scares you most about being honest?*

_____
_____
_____
_____
_____
_____
_____
_____

* *This question was already asked in the last journal moment, but it is necessary to ask again: What situation(s) or circumstance(s) has you feeling hopeless and weighed down under a blanket of darkness? Answer honestly.*

_____
_____
_____
_____
_____

Honestly share your thoughts and emotions surrounding this situation with God and with yourself. What emotions are you feeling right now? Do not censor yourself. Be completely honest.

※ *Is this time of honesty illuminating anything surprising? Anything that you did not realize you were carrying around?*

_____

_____

_____

_____

_____

_____

_____

Honesty is hard. You may find you need to hang out at this step for a bit. Sometimes truth reveals itself all at once…sometimes bits and pieces surface over time. No matter how it is disclosed, please know that it is okay. Take a breath. It is part of the process.

STEP 3

TRUST

"The glue that holds all relationships together--including the relationship between the leader and the led--is trust, and trust is based on integrity."

~Brian Tracy

STEP 3

<u>A TIME OF TRUST</u>

I struggled with trust for many years. Being molested and raped at age 5 thrusted me into a very adult world at far too tender of an age. Consequently, my go-to responses for survival were suspicion and distrust. And while I considered myself loyal and trustworthy, I did not believe others to be. But for a relationship to work, the trust must be a two-way street. It is arrogant and self-elevating to be involved in a relationship with the confidence that you yourself can be trusted but not the other person. And I do not mean when the other person proves they are not trustworthy…it is understandable to withhold trust in those cases. What I mean is when overall distrust of others with whom you are in relationship is your general rule.

You may be wondering what trust has to do with hope. Hope is an anchor…firm, secure, strong, and **trustworthy**. It keeps us tethered and tightly bound to God, His word, and His promises.

> *"This hope is a strong and trustworthy anchor for our souls. It leads us through the curtain into God's inner sanctuary."*
> *Hebrews 6:19, NLT*

For hope to be attained, trust must be cultivated. Trust is the confident reliance on the integrity of a person or thing. Read that again. *Trust is the confident reliance on the integrity of a person or thing*. Meaning trust requires integrity.

Integrity is the practice of being consistently honest. Not just honest…but consistently honest. That means honesty at **all** times. Committing to the practice of being consistently honest with God and with yourself is a display of integrity. This demonstration of integrity by unfailingly operating in honesty establishes trust.

In addition to integrity, trust — particularly trust in God — requires surrender. God wants us to cast all our cares and worries on Him. He wants us to trust Him with the bad times in our lives as well as the good. He wants us to hand over our shortcomings and failures as well as our successes and victories. God wants us to know He is our haven…our refuge…our safe place to fall. He wants us to be secure in the belief that we can close our eyes, spread our arms out wide and fall backwards knowing He will always catch us.

Surrender to God is beautiful, but it is not always easy. It requires faith. It is an exercise in trust. Just as an athlete lifts weights to become stronger, the more you surrender, the deeper your trust will become.

Knowing we can trust God…having the confident assurance that He will never leave nor forsake us…there is hope in that!

> *"The Lord himself goes before you and will be with you; he will never leave you nor forsake you. Do not be afraid; do not be discouraged."*
> *~Deuteronomy 31:8, NIV*

It takes trust to follow. It takes trust for us to surrender to and be led by God and His Son Jesus Christ. And while trusting is difficult, if we allow ourselves to depend on Him, we are promised light. Trusting in God drives out the darkness. Trusting in His integrity assures us we will be able to capture glimmers of hope.

> *"When Jesus spoke again to the people, he said, 'I am the light of the world. Whoever follows me will never walk in darkness but will have the light of life.'"*
> *~John 8:12, NIV*

As we journey down dark and uncertain roads, trust must be our travel companion. Placing confidence in an unknown outcome feels both frightening and overwhelming because not only must we trust God, but we must also trust the path He has set before us.

> *Commit your way to the Lord;*
> *trust in him and he will do this:*
> *He will make your righteous reward shine like the dawn, your vindication like the noonday sun.*
> *~Psalm 37:5-6, NIV*

It seems like a daunting task, but every moment spent sitting in the dark forest of your situation, late at night with nothing but an empty jar, is worth it. Because before long, a glimpse of brightness will be right in front of you…a firefly…a righteous reward. And all you will have to do is open your jar and catch it.

Footsteps of the Wind

Softly and sweetly
    you tiptoed into my life
      so unexpectant
      so pleasant
a refreshing change
a clean breeze
with gentle creaks
…like footsteps of the wind

Fearlessly and abandonedly
    I followed you lovingly
      so enraptured
      so captivated
head-over-heels
never the same
my heart a willing welcome mat
…for footsteps of the wind

Unpredictable and impractical
    your breath caressed my heart
    and my plans were disassembled
a welcomed shift
a break from the norm
my life interrupted
…by footsteps of the wind

Smoothly and melodious
your rhythm flows over me like waves of the sea
    a push

    a pull
and I'm dancing
and swaying
…with footsteps of the wind

Faintly and thunderous
    your presence is both tangible and illusive
    unseen
    but so deeply felt
I am delightfully enchanted
magically captivated
…by footsteps of the wind

Swiftly and vanishing
    your essence begins to fade
    quickly dissipating
    trickling off in many directions
without a word, you walk away
…like footsteps of the wind

Can I Trust You with My Voice?

My voice is a compilation
Of complex sounds
That reveal my identity
I don't know if I can trust you with them
I don't know if I can even trust me

If I sing you a song
Will you hold each note
Carefully in your hands?
Or will my expressions fall to the ground
If it's something you don't understand?

Mine is one
of a billion whispers
And a hundred million screams
But will you hear its singularity
And validate my dreams?

I taste the sweetness
Of every syllable
As the sounds pour from my lips
When they reach your cup will they be bitter?
Can I trust you to take a sip?

When quiet words rest upon my face,
In my dress,
Or the way that I walk
Will you take the time to hear from within,
When I'm too downtrodden to talk?

As I exquisitely compose
An orchestral masterpiece
And place it in your command
Will you admire the contradicting sounds
And gracefully strike up the band?

Are you bold enough
To come out of the shallow
And navigate the roar of my waves?
Can I trust you with the depths of my soul?
Can I possibly emerge unscathed?

As I honestly speak
each piece of truth
fireflies spark and rejoice
I need to capture their tiny glimmers
But can I trust you with my voice?

Me, Myself, and I

Trusting me, myself, and I
Honestly interrupting every secret lie
Pulling back the veil and exposing me
Experiencing my authenticity

Looking at me, myself, and I
Knowing where every mystery hides
Finding the keys that unlock hope
Believing in me and my ability to cope

Befriending me, myself, and I
Seeing gentleness in my own eyes
Giving faith permission to abide
Knowing in myself I can trust and confide

Loving me, myself, and I
Giving attention to every tear I have cried
Opening the book tucked away on the shelf
Realizing I can trust me with myself
This is Me, Myself, and I

A Guided Journal Moment:

ON TRUST

For any relationship to be considered successful, there must be a bond of trust. Trust is generally withheld when some breach of confidence has occurred. In my case — as shared previously in this section — my earliest and most damaging betrayal happened when I was molested and raped at the age of 5. But distrust can result from various causes.

Anytime we are disappointed, betrayed or let down by the actions of another, loyalty is called into question and the bond of trust is weakened. This sets the stage for future relationships. We learn from our experiences. And if our experiences teach us that there is pain associated with trusting others, then we will avoid that action to preserve and protect our own emotions.

We even run the risk of not trusting ourselves. Not trusting oneself can be the result of repeated poor choices, diminished self-esteem or, perhaps, an addiction. Whatever your source or sources of distrust are, it is important to identify them.

❦ *What was your earliest experience that resulted in feelings of distrust?*

_____
_____
_____
_____
_____
_____
_____
_____
_____
_____

❦ *If different than the one above, what was your most impactful situation that resulted in feelings of distrust?*

_____
_____
_____
_____
_____
_____
_____
_____
_____
_____
_____

❦ *Lies, deception, manipulation and rejection play a large part in our decisions to withhold trust. Take a moment and consider all the instances/relationships in which you chose to withhold trust. Did any or all these issues play a factor for you? Is there one that stands out most? Is there a negative attribute not listed that also had an undesirable impact?*

_____
_____
_____
_____
_____
_____
_____
_____
_____

❦ *Have you ever felt, or do you currently feel, unable to trust yourself? If yes, why?*

_____
_____
_____
_____
_____

- *What do you fear most when it comes to trusting others?*

  _____
  _____
  _____
  _____
  _____

- *What do you fear most when it comes to trusting yourself?*

  _____
  _____
  _____
  _____
  _____

- *What do you fear most when it comes to trusting God?*

  _____
  _____
  _____
  _____
  _____

- *When it comes to developing a trusting relationship with God, not only does it require integrity, but also surrender. Do you trust God? Are you fully surrendered to Him?*

  _____
  _____
  _____

Use the space below to list every hurt, pain, hardship, blessing, gift, talent, relationship, career, idea, plan, etc. List everything concerning you and surrender it all in prayer.

_____
_____
_____
_____
_____
_____
_____
_____
_____
_____
_____
_____
_____
_____
_____
_____
_____
_____
_____
_____
_____
_____

STEP 4

PATIENCE

"Hope is patience with the lamp lit."

~Tertullian

STEP 4

A TIME OF PATIENCE

Patience is one of the most difficult character traits to cultivate and develop. Being patient with God, with your circumstances, with others, and with yourself is a juggling act that takes practice and finesse. During every uncertain time in my life, be it something small or grand, I have had to muster, exercise and display patience. And, honestly speaking, I have not always succeeded. Essentially, patience is waiting. More specifically, patience is waiting *well*.

Over the years, I have learned that there are lessons in the wait. The wait can be equated to a forced stillness that requires you to position yourself in the classroom of life, receive a lesson and pass a test. And there is a consequence if you do not pass. That consequence: You will be directed to the same class, sit through the same lesson, retake the same test. Repeatedly. As many times as necessary.

Life is a tough teacher. But the one thing a tough teacher values most is a willing student. When we show up with a positive attitude and a desire to do the work, it is as if the teacher hands us the answer key. And that answer…Perspective! When we show up willingly, our perspective on the waiting shifts. We begin to value the wait. Consequently, something amazing occurs: Patience is developed. You cannot develop patience in any area without first having a proper perspective.

Life has thrown many courses in patience my way. I can vividly recall the agony I felt as my husband and I held our breaths while one of our twin sons had major abdominal surgery at 5 weeks old. It felt as though time was deliberately standing still, taunting me as I anxiously scanned the clock on the wall and paced in and out of his hospital room. That surgery would be the first of two. That hospital stay…the first of many. As time passed and we learned more about his illness, our perspectives shifted, and our patience grew. His condition developed great stamina and fortitude within us.

I wish I could say I retained everything that particular lesson in patience tried to impart. I did not. Nor did I learn everything regarding patience from every situation prior to or after that ordeal. But I did learn to practice it like an art.

The art of waiting well—waiting in patience—for a desired outcome that you cannot yet see is at the heart of capturing hope in your life. As phase four, it is the centermost stage in this 7-step process. Once you've mastered this step, you will not only develop a deeper appreciation for Positioning (Step 1), Honesty (Step 2) and Trust (Step 3), but you will also find it easy to glide through steps 5, 6 and 7…Healing, Courage and Expectation.

> *"But if we hope for what we do not see, we wait for it with patience."*
>
> Romans 8:25

"Rejoice in hope, be patient in tribulation, be constant in prayer."
Romans 12:12

Patience is key. It is the centerpiece. It is the anchor — the element that provides weight, foundation, and connection for this entire process.

Remember catching fireflies as a child? This step can be equated to the moment you are in the dark and you see that first flash of a firefly in the distance. And you know it is about to be spectacular!

I'll Dance

(Poem originally published in "The Belief in Wings" Donloyn LeDuff Gadson)

When you gaze upon my withered skin

Casting judgments

As if you know where I've been,

I'll Dance…

    Even Then, I'll Dance

When my peculiar stillness makes you jeer

Scoffing my intelligence

Instilling fear

I'll Dance…

    Even Then, I'll Dance

When you say nothing I touch will ever thrive

In your eyes I am barren

But inside I remain alive

I'll Dance…

    Even Then, I'll Dance

When life's challenges have beat me down

Unloved and unwanted
Crying tears of a clown

I'll Dance…
    Even Then, I'll Dance

When the forces working against me, devise a treacherous scheme
The elements, in all their grandeur, become my enemies

When the sun burns, beaming down, upon my weathered and blistered flesh
In this scorching, fiery furnace, I flail about and thresh

When the wind joins in the pounding, blowing, throwing, hurling
Causing a sandstorm of pain and hurt, and the oppression has me whirling

When the tide steps in, with its constant phases
Rising, drowning me, falling, exposing me, confusing me with all these changes

When the waves take center stage, crashing and thrashing against me
I retreat far within my twisted dry skin, in my sanctuary I hide deeply

When the sand shifts beneath my feet, bringing me instability
When I dig in deeper, holding on tighter, despite the uncertainty

I'll Dance…
    Even Then, I'll Dance

It's my toughened exterior that has allowed me to endure
Because of my hurts, I'm stronger
My heart is powerful; my soul triumphant
I know defeat no longer

The beauty, love and joy in my heart
Create a harmonious symphony
The trumpets and harps of angels collide
I dance as they serenade me
As I sway, spin and arabesque with each test
The trials become so easy

Throw at me what you will, do to me as you wish
Your doubt can no longer defeat me

I'll Dance…
    Even Then, I'll Dance

Even though the sun with its powerful rays
Burns me with its heat
When the hard day is done, I am granted reprieve
The torture stops, it retreats

The moon appears and cools my burns
Bringing with it twinkles of promise
Giving me time to dance with my dreams
A hope for a better tomorrow

In the morning, the sun will undoubtedly return
Bringing with it every conspirator
But I'll be waiting, with grace and elegance
Me, the beautiful dancer…

And I'll Dance…
    Even Then I'll Dance

my little light

anxiously waiting covered in night
grasping, fumbling, no calm in sight
perseverance, testing, focused fight
I'll just shine my little light

the waiting tests my will and might
developing patience deep as daylight
changes take place as I draw, and I write
magnified intensity from my little light

searching for the words to recite
a flood of emotions begins to incite
trying to say it all just right
trying to tell you about my little light

mine is but a little light
in a dark, dim world full of fright
harnessing my lumens to join the fight
'cuz even the smallest lights shine bright

my little light, blazing bright
one of a zillion stars in the night
brilliance unobscured, a vivid sight
following the glow of my little light

one in a billion twinkling lights

CATCHING FIREFLIES

one in a million lanterns in flight
one in a trillion sparkling sights
one in quadrillion shimmering nights

drawing its brilliance from The One True Light
set ablaze and free, a wild firelight
streaking the sky like a meteorite
patiently shining…my little light

A Guided Journal Moment:

ON PATIENCE

As stated previously, patience is the art of waiting well. But to wait well, there must be self-control. Controlling how you respond or react to challenges is indicative of your level of patience.

With patience, there will be tests. Tests that appear as daily irritations and frustrations. Tests that appear as a whining child, a difficult husband, an inconsiderate neighbor, or a lazy co-worker. Tests that appear as a 5-week-old infant undergoing surgery to correct a life-threatening condition.

Whether navigating something as simple as congested city streets or as heavy as personal trauma, we do not always recognize the tests. We get so caught up in what is happening that we do not always consider why it is happening. Therefore, it is imperative to pause before responding. Great patience lies in that pause. Pausing allows us to consider the possibility that what we are up against could be a lesson. That pause presents you with a choice. The choice to grow in patience or the choice to sit through the test again.

- *Consider the dark situation you are currently facing. Are you waiting well? Are you seizing the opportunity to display patience?*

_____
_____
_____
_____
_____
_____
_____
_____

- *If you have grown weary in your waiting, what are some ways you can respond differently?*

_____
_____
_____
_____
_____
_____
_____
_____
_____
_____

Pretend your situation is a dark forest and the hope and light you are seeking are fireflies. You are quietly positioned, ready to catch these small glimmers of hope. What are these fireflies in your circumstance? What do they look like? What little bits of hope and light are you believing to catch? (For example, if your situation is unemployment, perhaps you are hoping for an interview or a response to an inquiry.) Be specific about the fireflies you wish to catch. Remember Romans 8:25..."But if we hope for what we do not see, we wait for it with patience."

_____
_____
_____
_____
_____
_____
_____
_____
_____
_____
_____
_____
_____

STEP 5

HEALING

"You are the hero of your own story."

~Joseph Campbell

STEP 5

<u>A TIME OF HEALING</u>

God is the Father and Creator of all that is seen and unseen. He is all-knowing, all-present, and all-powerful. There is nothing and no one mightier than He. This truth makes the above mention by Joseph Campbell seem self-centered, self-glorifying and off-base, at best. However, it may surprise you that the above quote is neither of those things. It is accurate and holds the key to unlocking so many treasures that God has for us.

God is the most powerful being there ever was or will be, and His Son, Jesus Christ, is our Lord and Savior. No doubt about it. But there is one thing that possesses the ability to stop the divine power of God's Will in our lives. And that thing is the human will.

Human will — our God-given freedom to choose — is the most powerful force in our lives. And because of that power, you and I are the heroes of our own stories. I do not say that flippantly as if to suggest we are greater or more powerful than God. I say that to express that God has greatness He wants to release in our lives, but it all hinges upon us willingly partnering with Him on our journeys.

Let me clarify. There are times when God will place certain people, places and circumstances in our paths designed to bless, protect, or provide for us. Those are times when we receive His grace. In those instances, our consent is not needed. However, before God does anything in our lives that requires our full participation, we must willfully put ourselves in the position for that thing to happen. He will not force us into partnering with Him. He will not move against our wills. It is our choice to follow the calling and the anointing He has placed within each of us. It is our choice to boldly face situations where we need His guidance and direction. It is our choice to recognize the giants in our lives, take them on, and slay them. It is also our choice to heal and to be healed.

We are each called to embark upon our own hero's journey. That journey is a journey of healing. And healing requires participation. Therefore, it is up to each of us to decide if we want to heal or receive healing. It is an individual choice to begin the process of healing from old hurts, wounds, bitterness, offense, anger, pain, and rejection.

Healing is a time of exploration. It is a time to begin excavating and digging up buried thoughts, feelings, and emotions. Uncovering the skeletal remains of past traumas and disappointments can be a harrowing experience. But the heart is strong. It is a warrior. And it has everything it takes to be the hero. All through the power of choice. All by exercising the power of its will.

Healing is a crucial point in the process of capturing hope. There is no possibility of hope without implementing the element of healing. And healing begins with forgiveness. Forgiveness of others, forgiveness of self, and forgiveness of God. If we can position our hearts to forgive, then we can receive healing from the hurt and bitterness from past pain and trauma. Our emotional wounds block our ability to believe in the prospect of a brighter tomorrow.

"Get rid of all bitterness, rage and anger, brawling and slander, along with every form of malice. Be kind and compassionate to one another, forgiving each other, just as in Christ God forgave you."

Ephesians 4:31-32, NIV

After my miscarriage, I needed healing. And not only healing from the loss, but also healing from some lingering past hurts of which I was unaware. Forgiveness had to take place. I had to forgive others. I had to forgive myself. And I had to forgive God. It was overwhelming. But remember…The heart is strong.

I could have chosen to remain in that place of hurt and desolation. I could have chosen to continue to carry the residual hurts from past disappointments. Instead, I made the willful decision to be the hero of my own story. I chose light, hope, forgiveness, and healing. I chose to partner with God and allow Him to release His goodness into my situation. I chose to embark upon the journey and do the work. I surrendered my will over to the plans of God, and He escorted me from darkness to light. And I know He will do the same for you.

I Set This Day Before You

I set this day before You

Like a blank canvas

An empty sheet

A white space, an expanse

Open and ready

Open to possibilities

Unbridled and fully surrendered

Allowing you to freely craft something beautiful

I set this day before You

Ready to be impressed

Embossed

Written

Scribbled

Doodled

Scripted

Ready to be painted

Colored

Crafted and drawn

Drawn on and drawn in

Drawn into You

I set this day before You

Set it high upon your easel

Make it a masterpiece

Add colors

Bright colors, vibrant colors

Colors that bleed one into the other

Colors that hemorrhage hues never before seen

Let the creative blood cover me

Let Your Mighty finger be the paintbrush of Your Glory

The pen, the pencil, the crayon

Write, illustrate and mark on me

Mark my life with Your Glory

Or leave me black and white

Plain

Simple, easy

At the mercy of the onlookers' imaginations

Using me to prompt the colors of their minds

Causing them to think and explore

To fill in the deliberate white spaces with their own creative thoughts

Open to interpretation

Each eye seeing something different

Beholding that which he or she needs most

Beholding a healing designed uniquely for them

A creative healing only You can craft

When It Rains…

When it rains…
    do not be afraid
    it is cleansing
the rain flows and beats on my cheeks
it cleanses me
cleanses my heart and my mind
and the earth beneath my feet,
the place upon which I stand,
    the space I take,
the piece and peace of the planet to which I tend,
    my area to water and nourish
    my soul to quench
    my garden to grow

When it rains…
    do not hide
    it provides protection
there is a cover of clouds
shielding me
from the beautiful, violent rays of the sun
giving me a quiet solitude,
a private shade,
    a sanctuary for my soul,
a place of peace,
    delicate serenity

    to contemplate the light
    and process its lessons

When it rains…
    do not fear the grumbles
    it pounds out truths
the thunderous might of voice
the power of words…
spoken boldly and confidently
that shake and rattle,
the foundations of lies and pain,
    the groans that worship and pray,
shifting atmospheres,
commanding sounds that bang and bound
and reverberate in the bones and souls
of all who are near…
    those with ears let them hear!

When it rains…
    do not be terrified
    it powers movements
electrifying strikes and impulses
burn down the hiding places built by fear
their fire cauterizes open wounds
their lasers remove the scars that remain
to intimidate me with reminders of old identity
    the bolts are energized,
magnificent light

their pulverizing heat
a weapon of mass destruction
leaving healing in its wake

When it rains…
    do not run
    its cycle is productive
GET CAUGHT UP!
    in this tornadic whipping
    of purpose
    motored and fueled by past pain
GET CAUGHT UP!
    in this twirling and whirling
    that mixes and blends a salve,
        a healing balm,
            the proper prescription,
                a remedy,
    prescribed by the Creator of the storm
GET CAUGHT UP!
    in divine cycles
    that spin up and spit out
    all that is unwanted
get dizzy and drunk
    as you circle and encircle
    and rotate around The Source…
    the center of it all
        and you can just let go
because The Force is a centrifuge

   holding you,
   upright,
   while every impurity
   is stripped away

When it rains…
   be ready
   it demands preparation
a kit well stocked for survival
   a revelatory flash of light,
   a source to recharge your weary battery,
   strong meat and living waters,
   nonperishables, everlasting life
they are only found in The Word
   "Brace yourself and batten the hatches!"
   "Board up your windows and doors!"
This Cat 5 is about to hit your life
its name does not matter
   ride it out, you will not die
find rest in its eye
in His Eye
and when it is done
there will be a freshness,
clean up will be needed,
but all will be restored
healed,
made new

When it rains…
   do not be confused
   it brings every emotion
feel them all
feel them big
feel them grand

When it rains…
   sometimes only a light drizzle
   sometimes torrential downpours
   flooding every area of my life
   sometimes it is refreshing
   a light mist that accompanies sunshine,
      warm skies,
          and rainbows

When it rains…
   it pours
When it rains…
   it heals
When it rains…
   it's me
When it rains…
   it's my tears…and they heal me

A Guided Journal Moment:

ON HEALING

During my time of healing from my miscarriage, I wrote. I wrote a lot of poetry. I journaled. And I drew. But mostly, I wrote. I wrote words that conveyed deep thoughts and emotions.

It has always been my practice to write and create expressive words and images that are sources of healing for my audience. Writing, to me, was a pathway to healing on which I would sprinkle proverbial breadcrumbs to lead my readers to a place of restoration.

But while I was writing after my loss, God revealed something profound to me. He showed me that the gifting He placed within me to escort others to healing was the key to my very own. He revealed that during our hardships, we should use the gifting and anointing He placed within each of us for ourselves…to help ourselves heal and process.

So, if God has given you the gift of song, then sing…worship…write the music…sing the songs He has placed in your heart. If He has gifted you to serve, then serve others. If He has gifted you to write, draw, encourage, dance, build — whatever — then do those things! As you honor and nurture the gift He has placed in you, it honors Him…it brings Him worship. Worship ushers in the presence of God. And where the presence of the LORD is, there is healing.

Encourage yourself! Tap into the hope and light on the inside by using the gift God has given you!

"And David was greatly distressed; for the people spake of stoning him, because the soul of all the people was grieved, every man for his sons and for his daughters: but David encouraged himself in the Lord his God."

1 Samuel 30:6, KJV

- *God has healing for you. But you are the hero who must first say "Yes." Are you willing to partner with Him on this journey of healing? Do you consent to His involvement in your healing process?*

_____

_____

_____

_____

_____

_____

_____

- *Examine your heart. Are there any areas of unforgiveness that remain? Even the smallest amount is too much.*

- *Now, examine your current situation. Is this time of darkness bringing up or reminding you of any old hurts or wounds? If yes, unforgiveness may be there.*

* *Now that you have identified potential areas of unforgiveness, you must repent. Ask God to forgive you for not completely forgiving others. Write a prayer to Him here:*

_____
_____
_____
_____
_____
_____
_____
_____
_____
_____
_____
_____
_____
_____
_____
_____
_____
_____
_____
_____

Now, it is your turn. Forgive God, forgive yourself, and forgive the person or persons who hurt, wounded, rejected, or offended you. Begin that process here. Declare, in prayer, that you forgive. Ask God to help you to completely forgive. Keep doing this until you have purged your heart of all unforgiveness. Believe that God will help you.

- *What gifting has God given you that you usually use to bless or encourage others? How can you use it to encourage yourself?*

_____
_____
_____
_____
_____
_____
_____
_____
_____

- *Commit to honoring that gift, daily. Multiple times a day, if possible. Each time you exercise that gift, record it here:*

_____
_____
_____
_____
_____
_____
_____
_____
_____

STEP 6

COURAGE

"Courage is the most important of all the virtues because without courage, you can't practice any other virtue consistently."

~Maya Angelou

STEP 6

A TIME OF COURAGE

From the moment you plunged into the pages of this book, you have been hit by and swept up in waves of courage. It has been here all along. Pushing, pulling, and tugging on you.

How so? Because it takes courage to do anything well.

In step 4 of this guide, I shared that patience is the anchor for this entire process. Well, if patience is the anchor, then courage is the undercurrent. Courage is the undertone of this entire book. It takes courage to position yourself (step 1). It takes courage to be honest (step 2). It takes courage to trust (step 3). It takes courage to demonstrate patience (step 4). It takes courage to heal (step 5). And it will take courage to open yourself up to the vulnerability of expectation (step 7). It takes courage to catch fireflies!

Interestingly, courage began long before these pages were written. It took courage for me to live through my own darkness that led to the revelation of these 7 actions. It took courage for me to catch my own fireflies, process the lessons, compile them, and write this book for you. And now, it takes courage for you — the reader — to invest time exploring these pages and working through the steps.

The reason it takes courage is because all these stages of capturing hope are frightening. It is terrifying to peel away at your own darkness until you uncover a layer of light.

Mark Zuckerberg once said, "It takes courage to choose hope over fear." You see, hope provides no guarantee. And because of that, fear is at the forefront of each of these stages waiting to intimidate and discourage you from moving forward in light. But do not believe its empty threats. Be courageous and choose hope. The light that hope brings is so much better than the dark, dreary dungeon of fear.

> *"Have I not commanded you? Be strong and courageous. Do not be frightened, and do not be dismayed, for the Lord your God is with you wherever you go."*
> *~Joshua 1:9, ESV*

Have courage throughout this process. The LORD will be with you in the dark of night as you wait to capture glimmers of hope.

I Hear the Wind

sitting here…
    I hear the wind.
    its sounds,
    its power,
    its irregularity

how it whips and whirls,
    dashes and dances,
    rips and runs

as I listen…
I can feel it.
    its cold touch,
    its cruel sharpness,
    cutting and chafing,
    pricking my skin,
    piercing my soul,
bringing confusion by kissing my cheeks and softly stroking my hair

I feel it hates me
but I know it loves me.

I think…

it's hard to tell

the only thing I know for sure

is that it's blowing…

raging,

stirring,

swirling,

both outside and inside of me.

its strength is overwhelming.

…and terrifying.

…and so, I close my eyes

I Stand

I stand

Seemingly alone, but never that

I stand

Showers from the skies and showers from my eyes
Penetrate and drench the ground around and beneath me

I stand

My feet sink just below the dark, lush, fertile soil
The lessons in this dirt desire to feed me

So I stand

Roots emerge from my soles
As my spirit and soul hunger and thirst
For the nutrients that only the ground can provide
And my roots grow deeper and deeper
And burrow yet deeper still
Forming an intricate, complex network
Of unseen channels and fiber optics
That will receive and transmit
Wisdom, knowledge, light and love
I create a profoundly connected underground sea
That intertwines and weaves through the earthen darkness
As I stand

I stand

Fusing together, my legs become one
I dare not run

Fear has no hold, no effect
No power over me
I am strength. Fortified.
My powerful exterior is matchless

I stand

Like a wall of courage
A fortress of faith
Impenetrable by doubt
Unphased and unbothered by the winds of change and uncertainty
Their breath only serves to fluff and style my royal crown
My beautifully verdant mane dances gracefully as they blow
They blow fiercely and ferociously

But I stand

Nourishment is sucked through my roots from the Spirit that permeates the ground
And its life-giving power is soaked
In and up my body
The strength and power travels from my legs and up my trunk
As my body forms a trunk
The energy so intense I can't help but shout and throw my arms up high
Like branches

As I stand

My Branches
They are extensions of my voice
Extensions of the dynamic intensity that pulsates throughout each cell
Extensions that bear witness to the essence that drums

The extraordinary rhythm that reverberates throughout my entire being
And with each thump
And with each expression of voice
More branches are created

I stand

As the ornate root system below me is mimicked and replicated above me

I stand

As my branches design an ornate labyrinth with a scope and range beyond my imagination

I stand

As I give way to this process

I stand

As I surrender to the growth and development

I stand

As legacy and longevity have their way with me

I stand

As a power and might outside of myself
Fashions, shapes and forms my strength of character

I stand

As I become

BOLD, yet gentle and nurturing

I stand

As I become
Persistent, determined, resilient and committed

Committed to the ground
Committed to this community
Committed to these plans and purposes
Committed to the fruit and flowers that come forth and
Dangle from the Horizon of Hope my branches create

I stand

As my arms become an awe-inspired awning
A great canopy that is a manifestation of the unseen network below me
Manifestations that the eyes can behold
Natural product of a spiritual seed
And all the while

I stand

A Guided Journal Moment:

ON COURAGE

I feel like I have always been courageous. At least to some degree. However, at the same time, I have had my fair share of fear. I guess it would be accurate to say there has been an ongoing tug-of-war between courage and fear in my life. I think that can likely be said for most.

During the summer of 2014, I had a significant experience with fear that seemed to paralyze me. I had begun working on a manuscript. It was initially intended to be more of a personal development book, but it eerily shifted into a memoir. The story took me to places I had not been in a long while—places that had been calling me…places I was ignoring.

I was being called to an adventure, to my hero's journey. But like the beginnings of all great heroes, fear overwhelmed me, and I refused the call. I closed that Word document and left my half-told story imprisoned on my hard drive.

At the start of 2015, God stepped in. He gave me my first "Word of the Year," and that word was Courage. I became a student of Courage. Although I felt like I always had been courageous to a degree, I began making the conscious decision to apply it deliberately and live it intentionally. Now, courage is at the center of my everyday living.

Fear loves comfort. But Courage disrupts that comfort. Comfort is a hiding place for fear. But Courage seeks to expose it. Being courageous means becoming uncomfortable. That discomfort is a part of restoring hope. It is a part of stepping out of darkness and into light.

After my miscarriage, I had a choice to make. The comfortability that anger, aggression, and solitude provided…or the courage that promised a bright future and a brilliant hope. I chose the latter.

> *Consider the darkness that has been looming over you. Are you willing to get uncomfortable to bring light to it?*

You have been walking in courage since you opened the pages of this book. What is one courageous thing you can do right now to move away from your comfort zone and closer to a place of hope? For example, is there a conversation you can have with someone? Is there a truth you can admit? Is there something God has been calling you to do that you have been avoiding? What is that thing? What is that thing that will disrupt your comfort zone?

_____

_____

_____

_____

_____

_____

_____

_____

_____

_____

_____

_____

_____

_____

_____

_____

Now that you have identified that thing (because there is always one thing that we can do to move out of our comfort zones), write out an action plan to carry it out.

Look over your action steps. Be sure they are in proper order. Now, confront fear by taking the first step!

_____
_____
_____
_____
_____
_____
_____
_____

STEP 7

EXPECTATION

"There is no medicine like hope, no incentive so great, and no tonic so powerful as expectation of something tomorrow."

~Orison Swett Marden

STEP 7

<u>A TIME OF EXPECTATION</u>

There are so many cynical viewpoints and ideas surrounding the concept of expectation. I have often heard it said that it is wise to keep your expectations low to ensure you will not be disappointed. I have also heard the argument that we should not live up to the expectations of another, nor should we require others to live up to ours. While it is indeed unfair to place unrealistic demands on others, there is nothing unacceptable about creating an optimistic atmosphere for yourself and your own personal circumstances. Living in a state of anticipation for a desired, positive outcome is a sign of a healthy, well-adjusted person.

Let us examine the following scriptures:

For I know the thoughts that I think toward you, saith the Lord, thoughts of peace, and not of evil, to give you an expected end.

~Jeremiah 29:11, KJV

I know the plans that I have for you, declares Yahweh. They are plans for peace and not disaster, plans to give you a future filled with hope. ~Jeremiah 29:11, NOG

For this reason I am telling you, whatever things you ask for in prayer [in accordance with God's will], believe [with confident trust] that you have received them, and they will be given to you.

~Mark 11:24, AMP

The LORD wants us to have an expectation and a hope for a good outcome. He wants us to hope and expect light in our lives and in our situations. He tells us that He has plans for us, and those plans are meant to prosper us and lead to a hope-filled life.

If Jehovah says He has good things planned for us, is it unreasonable to wait in hope-filled expectation for the manifestation of those promises? No, it is not! In fact, if we know God has great things in store, and we know that we can petition Him in prayer and believe that it is already done, then we should sit in whatever darkness we are facing, learn the lesson it is teaching us, and allow it to shape us all while waiting expectantly for those sparkling glimmers of goodness and light!

Waiting in anticipation of fireflies to show up in your night season is not easy. It requires positioning, honesty, trust, patience, healing, and courage. Once you have journeyed through the first 6 phases of this guide, you are then ready and prepared to sit in expectation of a marvelous light. And that light is hope!

Do not be afraid to expect something brilliant!

The Hope Inside

Imagining the Hope inside
Takes my mind on an adventurous ride
Wild thoughts go up, down and slip and slide
Each time I imagine the Hope inside

Imagining the Hope inside
I am elevated and start to glide
Possibilities stretched out far and wide
Each time I imagine the Hope inside

Imagining the Hope inside
Every emotion begins to collide
Face fear head on or run and hide
Each time I imagine the Hope inside

Imagining the Hope inside
Child-like wonder on a carousel ride
The place where faith and the little girl reside
Each time I imagine the Hope inside

Imagining the Hope inside
It's the space creativity inhabits and abides
The place where inspiration is tested and tried
Each time I imagine the Hope inside

Imagining the Hope inside
A joyous river flows from the tears I've cried
Quenching the dry roots of dreams that once died
Each time I imagine the Hope inside

Imagining the Hope inside
Illuminates my path, a compass, a guide
It arrests the words of everyone who has lied
Each time I imagine the Hope inside

Imagining the Hope inside
My gait is upright, a confident stride
Shielded and protected with Faith by my side
Each time I imagine the Hope inside

Imagining the Hope inside
I cradle the promise in awe and wide-eyed
Forever to the blessing I am bound and tied
Each time I imagine the Hope inside

My Dream Sings to Me

My dream sings to me

In the night, in the day

When I am asleep

Or awake

Serenading me, wooing me

Coaxing me onto the dance floor

To dance

Pulling me into a game of cat and mouse

Chasing me

Then encouraging me to chase

Hunting me down

I hide. It seeks. It finds me. Every time.

And chains me with its song

Each chord binds me tighter

Every melody sweeter and more horrifying than the one before

The song is never ending

Its tune plays on a loop

in my heart

in my mind

in my ears

I see the notes, twirling and swaying in perfect motion

Before my eyes

The taste of its rich lyrics on my tongue

My dream sings to me

I cannot escape it

I plug my ears. It is there.

I close my eyes. It is there.

I close my mouth. Still there.

I pinch my nose and yet I still smell its melodic aroma

Wafting in the air

Its rhythm envelops me, and I feel its embrace

So, I give in

I give up and give in to its chimes

The giving in scares me

The song is big and intense and awesome in range

A pitch and an octave I have never before attained

But I give in

I give in because, between each verse,

Each line,

Each quarter note,

There is a promise

A promise sung just for me

But I must give in and sing along

And dance

In unison

In rhythm

With no fear

And no inhibitions

At night, in the day

When I am asleep or awake

My dream sings to me

My dream is from The LORD

And I do not want to miss it

A Guided Journal Moment:

ON EXPECTATION

It is interesting how a 7-step journey that was birthed out of the pain of miscarriage ends in a time of expectation. I love how God works in that way.

Before our loss, I was already expecting. I was expecting a new life. I was anticipating all that comes with pregnancy and a newborn baby. I was preparing for the upcoming changes to our family. I was looking forward to the promise of hope and making myself ready to receive it all. But things abruptly changed for me. All I was hoping for faded away. And in its place, all that remained was the exact opposite.

But as I began to work through my darkness, I began to hope again. New expectations started to fill my heart. I began to ready myself to receive these new promises and possibilities. Then, an important realization washed over me: We cannot just sit and wait for the promise; we must make preparation while we are in expectation!

Although my expectation of a healthy baby had ended in disappointment, that time showed me that we must prepare. Our preparation for the expectation is a display of faith. And faith requires action. We must be actively engaged and committed to that which we are expecting. God is not a magician who is going to wave a wand and then, poof, everything we were hoping for appears.

For example, if you are expecting to receive a book deal, you do not twiddle your thumbs and do nothing until a book deal magically lands in your lap. No. You write the book! You write query letters. You prepare. You make room in your life for that promise. This is true for anything we are expecting.

- *Look beyond the difficulties or darkness that may be around you. What are you expecting?*

_____
_____
_____
_____
_____
_____
_____
_____
_____

How will you actively engage with this expectation? What preparations will you make to ready yourself for its arrival?

CATCHING FIREFLIES

OPEN JARS

"Every object, every being…is a jar full of delight."

~Rumi

OPEN JARS

You made it. You have journeyed your way through poems, scripture, symbolism, stories, and prose. You have reflected on your circumstances, examined your heart, and responded to questions. You have willingly committed to Times of Positioning, Honesty, Trust, Patience, Healing, Courage, and Expectation. You may have taken a day for each step…a week…or even a month. The point is you made it! You should be seeing those glorious glimmers of hope! You should be seeing fireflies! And now, it is time to catch them!

I can recall taking a walk on a warm summer night while on vacation visiting my brother and his family. Fireflies were everywhere. It was a beautiful sight. I hurried back to the house, got jars from my sister-in-love, collected my children and nephew, and whisked them away on an exciting adventure to find light in the darkness.

As we stood still in the dark of night, anticipating the next magical flash, our jars were open. Open, awaiting the arrival of a tiny twinkle. Open and ready to receive the light.

Friend, if you have not realized it by now, you are the jar. We are all jars. And we must be open and ready to receive the light. We must have our hearts and minds open with plenty of room for the treasure God wishes to place within. The glorious, brilliant knowledge of Him through His son Christ Jesus is that treasure. That is the light!

And the precious beauty of all this is that God reveals bits and pieces of this amazing light in small glimmers. These tiny flickers of hope are whirling around and within you, waiting to be seen and captured.

"For God, who said, 'Let brilliant light shine out of darkness,' is the one who has cascaded his light into us – the brilliant dawning light of the glorious knowledge of God as we gaze into the face of Jesus Christ. We are like common clay jars that carry this glorious treasure within, so that the extraordinary overflow of power will be seen as God's, not ours. Though we experience every kind of pressure, we're not crushed. At times we don't know what to do, but quitting is not an option. We are persecuted by others, but God has not forsaken us. We may be knocked down, but not out."

2 Corinthians 4: 6-9, TPT

The dark season you are experiencing is just that…a season. It will not crush or overtake you. Not when you know your source of hope and light. You may not know exactly what to do, but do not quit. Do not give up on hope.

When times are at their darkest, that is when we need hope most.

Open your eyes. See the glimmers of light shimmering around you. Are you ready? Take a deep breath. Remove the lid. Open your heart and mind. Open your jar and start *Catching Fireflies*!

www.ingramcontent.com/pod-product-compliance
Lightning Source LLC
Chambersburg PA
CBHW060539100426
42743CB00009B/1575